MW00904293

THE ENCHANTED WALK
THROUGH THE WHEEL OF THE YEAR

BY CECILY RAVENWOOD

As a small, independent author and book creator, honest reviews are always appreciated! Thanks, and I hope this brings you as much joy as I had in creating it.

I HOPE YOU SEE
THE MAGIC IN ALL
OF THE SEASONS.

Magick can be found in every day of the year.

The Earth slowly travels around our Sun, tilting towards or away from the light, and all living things are affected by this celestial dance.

The seasons of the year exist because of the movement of our world around the sun. Many of the earth's natural processes work with the change of sunlight, like when the tree nuts fall in autumn, freeze in winter, and then grow the next spring.

Long ago, when people lived by the light of the sun, moon and fire, they marked special solar events, called solstices or equinoxes, with celebrations. These holidays had many different names across different cultures but were very similar because they were based on the natural changing of the seasons. They marked activities like putting herds of animals out to pasture or harvesting certain crops.

These festivals are still celebrated all over the world by pagans. Together, the celebrations make the Wheel of the Year.

Celebrating the changing seasons of the year is still important, even though not every family has crops to tend or animals to herd. Using nature as inspiration for holidays keeps us connected to the rhythms of Mother Earth. And remaining connected to our world is an important part of protecting our environment.

Yule
Imbolc
Ostara
Beltane
Litha
Lughnasadh
Mabon
Samhain

Because the Wheel of the Year is a circle, people can celebrate the beginning of the year when they want. Some celebrate the beginning of the year at Yule time, which is how modern calendars also mark the new year. Some pick the Witch's New Year, on Samhain.

I choose Ostara because it marks the beginning of the regrowth of plants. Although Imbolc also has small signs of spring, Ostara is the start of plant growth in my area.

Your family's traditions and beliefs will be important when deciding when to celebrate the new year.

SPRING

The natural year begins with the new growth and new life of spring. Like you and I began life as tiny new humans, nature begins the year with seeds sprouting and new babies of all kinds!

Every place experiences the beginning of Spring differently. In some areas, spring is obvious, because snow melts and it gets warmer each day. For those that live in places that are warm all year round, it might be harder to notice spring's arrival.

OSTARA

SPRING EQUINOX

NORTHERN HEMISPHERE - ON OR AROUND MARCH 20

SOUTHERN HEMISPHERE - ON OR AROUND SEPTEMBER 20

Ostara takes place on the spring equinox. An equinox is a special day because it means that the day and the night are equal amounts of time. This only happens two times a year!

After a long winter of darkness, Ostara welcomes longer and warmer days in the sunshine. It is a celebration of the plants that turn the earth green and the new baby animals.

A great way to celebrate the new beginnings that Ostara represents would be to find a new hobby or interest to get into.

BELTANE

While Beltane is not officially the start of summer, it marks the start of summer activities. Long ago, this was when people brought their herd animals to summer pastures or make offerings for a successful growing season for their crops.

A great way to celebrate Beltane would be to start a small garden. This could be as small as getting a new houseplant or starting a window herb garden, or as big as making a new flower garden outside for the bees and butterflies.

SUMMER

Summer is a beautiful time of year. The babies in the fields and forests are playing about, the bees and other pollinators are buzzing, and the sun shines brightly on it all.

Summer is also important because it is the natural time to grow and care for food crops. The sun and warmth make outdoor growing possible.

LITHA

SUMMER SOLSTICE
NORTHERN HEMISPHERE - ON OR AROUND JUNE 21
SOUTHERN HEMISPHERE - ON OR AROUND DECEMBER 21

Litha is the celebration of the summer solstice or the first official day of summer. The summer solstice is the longest day of the year. There is no other day all year long that has more daytime than Litha!

Because it marks the sunniest day of the whole year, Litha festivities often center around the sun. It is also the last hurrah before the hard work of the fast-approaching harvest season.

Litha is best celebrated with gratitude for the sun. Activities that would be great on LItha might be going on a hike in the sunshine or making a jar of sun tea or lemonade. Water activities like swimming or canoeing are also a great way to celebrate the longest day of the year.

AUTUMN

Autumn, or fall, was important to people of the past because it was time to harvest their food for the winter. As summer changes to autumn, grains must be harvested, followed by root vegetables and gourds.

In some parts of the world, the trees slowly turn color and then lose their leaves as the temperature grows colder. The grasses turn to gold in the fields. The migrating birds will slowly start to move to their winter homes.

Long ago, as harvests winded down and cupboards were filled with food, the last outdoor celebrations were held. People knew that the snows of winter would prevent outdoor festivities from happening until spring arrived again.

LUGHNASADH

HALFWAY BETWEEN SUMMER SOLSTICE AND AUTUMN EQUINOX
NORTHERN HEMISPHERE - AUGUST 1
SOUTHERN HEMISPHERE - FEBRUARY 1

Lughnasadh is the first of the three autumn harvest celebrations. This holiday marks the harvest of grains and other early crops, like fruits.

Lughnasadh is a celebration of gratitude for the grain harvest. Some activities to mark this special time might be to bake, support your local farmers' market, or cook a festive meal with bread, grain, corn, and fruit as the main ingredients.

MABON

AUTUMNAL EQUINOX
NORTHERN HEMISPHERE - ON OR AROUND SEPTEMBER 21
SOUTHERN HEMISPHERE - ON OR AROUND MARCH 21

Mabon festivities take place on the autumnal equinox. This means that for the second time in the year, the day and the night are equal.

Mabon is also celebrated during the harvest of later autumn crops, like root vegetables and gourds. Like Lughnasadh, Mabon is also meant to show gratitude for what is collected in preparation for winter.

Mabon activities to mark the autumn equinox might be showing gratitude by donating what you no longer need or providing community service. Your family might also prepare a feast to celebrate the autumnal equinox or take a nature walk to see the first hints of autumn.

SAMHAIN

HALFWAY BETWEEN AUTUMN EQUINOX AND WINTER SOLSTICE

NORTHERN HEMISPHERE - OCTOBER 31 TO NOVEMBER 1

SOUTHERN HEMISPHERE - APRIL 31 TO MAY 1

Considered to be the witches' New Year, Samhain is an especially magickal holiday that falls halfway between the autumn equinox and the shortest day of the year. It is the last autumn harvest celebration and welcomes the darker days of winter.

Because Halloween borrows many customs from Samhain, a lot of Samhain activities might sound familiar.

Samhain is a holiday to honor your ancestors. You can do this by telling stories of your ancestors, or by having a meal in their honor. You may also choose to dress in a costume and visit family or neighbors for treats or food, to celebrate the last harvest of the year.

WINTER

Wintertime is a quieter time of year for many people in colder climates. Because the days are short and the nights are long in colder places, the winter season might be spent mainly indoors, playing with family.

Before electricity, this was even more the case, as winter travel at night was more dangerous.

Even though winter may be hard for these reasons, it is also a beautiful and necessary part of the natural world.

YULE

Yule is the celebration of darkness and light. It falls on the shortest day and longest night of the year. It is a celebration to welcome the return of the sun, and with it, longer days.

Because Yule is the darkest day of the year, many festivities include light, such as candles or string lights.

On Yule, your family could decorate a tree indoors. This helps to brighten up the darkness of the season by bringing in green life and light. Decorating the house is also a great way to bring some cheer to your home. Baking orange slices and stringing up cranberries is a natural way to decorate and can be shared with wildlife afterward if cotton string is used.

IMBOLC

HALFWAY BETWEEN WINTER SOLSTICE AND SPRING EQUINOX
NORTHERN HEMISPHERE - FEBRUARY 1
SOUTHERN HEMISPHERE - ON OR AROUND DECEMBER 21

Imbolc is a sweet celebration to mark the first signs of spring, though the winter still has its hold on much of the land. The cold winter nights are slowly shrinking, leaving more time for sunny days.

Imbolc is a celebration of the signs of spring. Take a nature walk to find signs of spring around your community. Family grownups may choose to have a bonfire to celebrate Imbolc. Spring cleaning is also a great way to sweep out the dust of winter and welcome the light of spring.

There are so many things you can do to celebrate your connection to the earth and the seasons, no matter what day of the year it is.

Take walks with a small grocery bag so that you can pick up any garbage you find.

Instead of throwing something away, find a way to reuse it or make it into artwork.

Find a way to notice nature every day. If something you see makes you happy, thankful, or excited, write in your journal about it, or tell someone you love.

About the Author

Cecily Ravenwood is an indigenous woman that lives in the North Woods with her three little ones, her partner, a dog, 2 cats, a gecko, and a bunch of fish. When she isn't homeschooling or taking care of animals, she loves to create, to be in the garden, and to explore the forest.

Made in United States
Troutdale, OR
12/09/2024

26173571R10026